Sikh Festivals
throughout the Year

Anita Ganeri

A⁺
Smart Apple Media

First published in Great Britain by Franklin Watts
96 Leonard Street, London EC2A 4XD

Franklin Watts Australia
45–51 Huntley Street, Alexandria NSW 2015
Copyright © 2003 Franklin Watts

Editor: Kate Banham, Designer: Joelle Wheelwright, Art Direction: Jonathan Hair, Picture
Research: Diana Morris, Map (p. 7): Aziz Khan, Faith Consultant: Rajinder Singh Panesar,
Bradford Interfaith Center

Published in the United States by Smart Apple Media
1980 Lookout Drive, North Mankato, MN 56003

U.S. publication copyright © 2004 Smart Apple Media
Printed in Hong Kong

Library of Congress Control Number: 2003104231

ISBN 1-58340-374-4

9 8 7 6 5 4 3 2 1

The publishers would like to thank the following for permission to reproduce photographs in
this book: Gordon Clements/Axiom, 25tr; B. Dhanjal/Trip, 22tr; Dinodia Photo Library, 26b;
Paul Doyle/Photofusion, 13t, 20t; Paul Gapper/World Religions Photo Library, 26t;
Arvind Garg/Corbis, 15tl; Prem Kapoor/World Religions Photo Library, 19b;
Christine Osborne/World Religions Photo Library, front cover, 10bl, 17t, 23t, 24t;
H. Rogers/Trip, 6c, 10tr,11c,16t,18r, 21t, 22bl, 25bl, 27t; Trip, 8b, 14t.

Contents

Words printed in **bold** are explained in the glossary.

Introduction

Sikhs are people who follow the religion of Sikhism. It began about 500 years ago in **Punjab** in northwest India. At that time, **Hinduism** and **Islam** were the main religions in India. But they were deeply divided, and many people felt left out. A holy man, Nanak, introduced the new religion of Sikhism, which taught tolerance and equality. He became the first Sikh **Guru**, or teacher. Today, there are about 14 million Sikhs. Most still live in India.

*The Golden Temple in **Amritsar**, India, is the center of the Sikh faith.*

Festival dates

Sikh festivals are traditionally based on the ancient Hindu lunar calendar. The lunar year is shorter than the solar year on which the Western calendar is based. To bring the two calendars into line, an extra month is added every few years. In 1999, a new Sikh calendar was introduced. It was called *Nanakshahi*, or Royal Nanak. It dates from 1469, the year of Guru Nanak's birth. (See page 28 for the names of the Hindu months and the names of the *Nanakshahi* months.) But the vast majority of Sikhs still use the Hindu lunar calendar to determine the timing of festivals.

Sikh beliefs

Sikhs believe that there is only one God. They hope to grow closer to God by remembering Him in everything they do, working hard, living honestly, and caring for others. The ideal of looking after others, without thought of reward, is very important to Sikhs. It is called **sewa**, or service. Another key belief is that everyone—man or woman, rich or poor—is equal in God's eyes. All religions lead to the same God, and all should be tolerated.

How Sikhs worship

A *Gurdwara* is a building where Sikhs meet to worship and learn more about their faith. The word *Gurdwara* means "gateway to the Guru." Any building can be a *Gurdwara* as long as it contains a copy of the **Guru Granth Sahib**, the Sikhs' holy book. In the *Gurdwara*, Sikhs listen to readings from the holy book, sing **shabads** (hymns), and say prayers. Afterwards, they share a meal, called **langar**. Sikhs take turns cooking and serving langar to show that everyone is equal

▲ *Sikhs worshipping in a* **Gurdwara** *in front of the Guru Granth Sahib.*

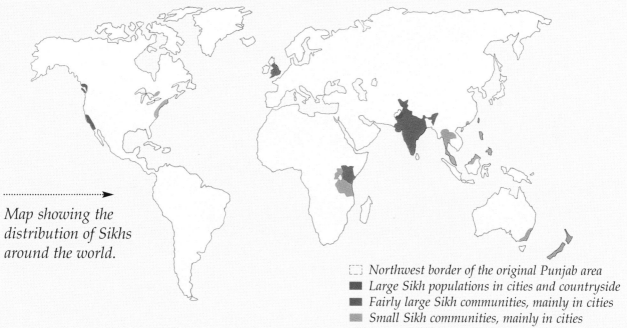

Map showing the distribution of Sikhs around the world.

☐ *Northwest border of the original Punjab area*
■ *Large Sikh populations in cities and countryside*
■ *Fairly large Sikh communities, mainly in cities*
■ *Small Sikh communities, mainly in cities*

Sikh festivals

There are two kinds of Sikh festivals: *gurpurbs* and *jore melas*. *Gurpurb* means "Guru's day." These festivals remember key times in the lives of the 10 Sikh Gurus, such as their birthdays and deaths. The word *jore* means "a gathering," and *mela* means "a fair." These festivals celebrate other great events from Sikh history. They are less serious occasions than *gurpurbs*, with fair rides, food, and dancing. Festivals are important for reminding Sikhs of their history and inspiring them to live good lives.

The Sikh Gurus

Guru Nanak was the first Sikh Guru. Before he died, he chose one of his followers to be Guru after him. For the next 170 years, Sikh beliefs were passed down through a line of Gurus. In the Punjabi language, the word *Guru* means "a teacher inspired by God." There are 10 human Gurus and the Guru Granth Sahib (see right). The Gurus teach Sikhs how to grow closer to God.

A painting showing the Sikh Gurus.

The 10 Gurus

This list gives the names of the 10 Sikh Gurus, with the dates of their births and deaths, and some of their main achievements.

1 **Guru Nanak (1469–1539)** was the first Guru of the Sikh religion. He taught the basic Sikh beliefs and established many Sikh customs, such as *langar*.

2 **Guru Angad Dev (1504–1552)** finalized *Gurmukhi*, the script in which the Guru Granth Sahib is written. The word *Gurmukhi* means "from the Guru's mouth."

3 **Guru Amar Das (1479–1574)** encouraged the Sikhs to gather together twice a year to celebrate the festivals of *Baisakhi* and *Divali*.

4 **Guru Ram Das (1534–1581)** founded the city of Amritsar in Punjab, the center of the Sikh faith. He also composed the *Lavan*, the Sikh wedding hymn.

5 **Guru Arjan Dev (1563–1606)** built the Harimandir (Golden Temple) in Amritsar (see page 6). He collected the Sikh sacred writings together to form the Guru Granth Sahib.

6 **Guru Hargobind (1595–1644)** encouraged the Sikhs to fight for what they believed in. He wore two swords, which stood for spiritual and worldly power.

7 **Guru Har Rai (1630–1661)** helped to spread the Sikh religion. He also set up hospitals that provided free medicine and treatment to everyone who needed it.

8 **Guru Har Krishan (1656–1664)** was only five when he became Guru. He is remembered for caring for the sick until he died of smallpox at the age of eight.

9 **Guru Tegh Bahadur (1621–1675)** helped the Hindus stand up to the Muslim Mughal emperor. The emperor later had him arrested and killed.

10 **Guru Gobind Singh (1666–1708)** was the last of the human Gurus. At the festival of *Baisakhi* in 1699, he set up the **Khalsa**, the Sikh community.

A Sikh worshipper reading from the
Guru Granth Sahib.

Guru Granth Sahib

When Guru Gobind Singh was close to death, he did not name a person to succeed him as Guru. Instead, he told the Sikhs that their Guru would be the Guru Granth Sahib, their holy book. The Guru Granth Sahib is made up of hymns, mostly composed by the Gurus. Sikhs believe it is the word of God and treat it with great respect.

Mool Mantar

The Mool Mantar prayer begins the Guru Granth Sahib. It was composed by Guru Nanak and sums up Sikh beliefs about God:

"There is only one God
Whose name is Truth
God the creator
Is without fear
Is without hate
Is timeless and without shape
Is beyond death, the enlightened one
And is understood through God's grace."

Guru Nanak's Birthday

In November, Sikhs all over the world remember the birthday of Guru Nanak, the first Sikh Guru. This is one of the most important times in the Sikh calendar. You can read about how Sikhs celebrate this festival on pages 12–13.

A painting of Guru Nanak, the first Sikh Guru and teacher of the Sikh religion.

A Gurdwara built in honor of Guru Nanak at his birthplace near Lahore in Pakistan.

Guru Nanak's birth

Guru Nanak was born in 1469 in the village of Talwandi, southwest of Lahore (now in Pakistan). His family were Hindus. From an early age, Nanak was deeply religious, and, according to Sikh stories, several events from his childhood made clear he was special. Once, he fell asleep while looking after some cattle, which wandered off and trampled a neighbor's crop of wheat. The neighbor was very angry, but Nanak told him not to worry. When the neighbor looked at his field again, the wheat was better than ever.

Vision of God

When Nanak was about 30 years old, he went down to the river to bathe as usual but did not come back home. His friends and family thought that he must have drowned. But three days later, Nanak returned. He said that he had been taken up into heaven and had seen God. God told Nanak to teach people how to live good and truthful lives. Nanak told his friends, "I know now that God is neither **Hindu** nor **Muslim**, so the path I shall follow is neither Hindu nor Muslim, but God's." From then on, Nanak was known as "Guru."

A Hymn by Guru Nanak

"I was an out of work minstrel.
God gave me work.
God gave me the order,
'Sing my praise night and day.'
God summoned the minstrel
to the divine court.
He bestowed on me the robe of
honoring God and singing
His divine praises."

A painting of Guru Nanak (with halo) and his friend Mardana (seated).

Travels and teachings

Guru Nanak gave up his job and possessions and became a wandering teacher. He taught that there is one God, and that everyone is equal in God's eyes. Guru Nanak often used poetry to explain these teachings. His verses were set to music by his faithful traveling companion, the Muslim musician Mardana.

When Guru Nanak was an old man, he settled in the village of Kartarpur in the Punjab. People came from far and wide to learn from him. Just before he died, Guru Nanak chose Guru Angad Dev to be his successor.

Birthday Celebrations

Every *gurpurb* festival (in honor of a Guru's birthday) is celebrated in a similar way, with a reading of the Guru Granth Sahib, services in the *Gurdwara,* and street processions.

Readers take turns reading from the Guru Granth Sahib.

Akhand Path

The most important part of a *gurpurb* is a reading of the Guru Granth Sahib from beginning to end. This is called an **Akhand Path**, which means "unbroken recitation." An *Akhand Path* is held in the *Gurdwara* and takes about 48 hours. It is timed to end early on the morning of the day of the festival. Readers work in teams, and no one reads for more than two hours at a time because the words must be clear. A backup reader is always ready to take over if someone gets sick.

Gurdwara service

During the *Akhand Path*, many Sikhs stop at the *Gurdwara* to listen for a while, then go home again. After the reading is completed, a service is held. There are talks about the meaning of the *gurpurb*, and hymns in praise of the Guru. At the end of every Sikh service, people share a sweet pudding called **karah parshad** (see page 17). The act of sharing is a way of showing that everyone is equal. Afterwards, *langar* is served.

A meal is served after every Sikh service.

↑ *Sikhs dressed as the* Panj Piare.

Street processions

In India and in other countries with large Sikh communities, there are processions through the streets to celebrate a *gurpurb*. The procession is led by five devout Sikh men who represent the **Panj Piare** (five beloved ones), who were the first members of the *Khalsa*, or Sikh community (see pages 20–21). They wear orange or yellow robes and turbans, as the *Panj Piare* wore. Behind them comes a beautifully decorated float that carries the Guru Granth Sahib. The congregation follows the float, singing hymns written by the Gurus and other holy men. People watching the procession are often given sweets or drinks as a way of joining in.

A Birthday Hymn

These lines are from the most popular shabad *sung at Guru Nanak's birthday. It is by a Sikh writer named Bhai Gurdas.*

"The merciful Lord heard the cries of humanity
And sent Guru Nanak to this earth.
He prayed to God in utter humility and gave the nectar of God's name to his followers.
In the dreadful Dark Age,
Guru Nanak sang God's praise.
The Guru established the Sikh religion and brought all people together.
He treated prince and pauper alike and his followers learned to bow in humility to each other.
He performed this unique act to teach humility to his followers.
Baba Nanak liberated people from the Dark Age and taught them God's true name.
Guru Nanak came to this world to save humankind."

Guru Tegh Bahadur

Another *gurpurb* takes place in November to mark the death of the ninth Guru, Guru Tegh Bahadur. Sikhs remember how, in 1675, Guru Tegh Bahadur gave up his life for the right to practice his religion freely. Sikhs believe that he is an example for all religions to follow. A person who dies for his or her faith is called a martyr, and his or her death is called **martyrdom**.

A painting of Guru Tegh Bahadur, whose death is marked in November.

The Guru dies for his faith

In Guru Tegh Bahadur's time, India was ruled by the Mughal Emperor Aurangzeb, who was a **devout** Muslim. Aurangzeb wanted to force all Hindus and Sikhs to become Muslims. Many Hindus were killed because they refused to give up their faith. A group of Hindu holy men came to ask Guru Tegh Bahadur for his help. They knew that he taught that everyone had the right to follow his or her own way of life. The Guru told the holy men to send a message to the emperor. The message said that if the emperor could persuade Guru Tegh Bahadur to convert to Islam, all Hindus would follow his example.

The emperor was delighted. He called the Guru to Delhi and offered him palaces and other riches if he became a Muslim. But the Guru refused. Furious, the emperor threatened him with torture. But still the Guru would not give up his faith. So the emperor had him tortured and beheaded.

Remembering the Guru

Like most *gurpurbs*, Guru Tegh Bahadur's death is remembered by holding an *Akhand Path*, saying prayers, singing hymns, and having street processions. This *gurpurb* is especially important in Delhi, the capital of India. This is where the Guru was put to death. A beautiful *Gurdwara* called the Sis Ganj Sahib Gurdwara has been built on the site of his execution.

The Sis Ganj Sahib Gurdwara in Delhi, India, the site of Guru Tegh Bahadur's martyrdom.

A *romalla*

When the Guru Granth Sahib is not being read, it is covered with a beautifully decorated cloth called a *romalla*. On special occasions, such as the completion of an *Akhand Path*, Sikhs make an offering of a *romalla* in the *Gurdwara*.

patterns, flowers, leaves, and Sikh symbols, such as the *Ik Onkar* (right), which means "There is only one God."

To make a romalla:

1. Cut a piece of brightly colored cloth about 40 inches (1 m) by 50 inches (1.25 m). Turn over the edges and sew or pin the hems down.

2. Sew or pin a length of gold ribbon around the edges of the cloth.

3. Decorate the cloth using fabric pens or paints. Draw geometric

Guru Gobind Singh's Birthday

The birthday of Guru Gobind Singh, the 10th Sikh Guru, falls in January. It is celebrated by Sikhs all over the world. Special celebrations take place in Patna, India, where Guru Gobind Singh was born.

A painting of the 10th Sikh Guru, Guru Gobind Singh.

A *Shabad* by Guru Gobind Singh

"Grant me this boon
O God, from Thy greatness.
May I never refrain
From righteous acts.
May I fight without fear
All foes in life's battle,
With confident courage
Claiming the victory!
May Thy glory be
Ever in my mind,
And my highest ambition be
Singing Thy praises.
When this mortal life
Reaches its end,
May I die fighting
With limitless courage!"

The life of Guru Gobind Singh

Guru Gobind Singh was born in 1666. He became Guru at the age of nine after the death of his father, Guru Tegh Bahadur (see pages 14–15). Guru Gobind Singh was a brilliant scholar and a brave warrior, and he had a kind and generous nature. He had to fight many battles to protect the Sikhs and their religious freedom. In 1699, at the festival of Baisakhi, he started the *Khalsa*, or Sikh community (see pages 20–21). Guru Gobind Singh did not name a human Guru to lead the Sikhs after him. Just before he died in 1708, he told the Sikhs to look to the Guru Granth Sahib for spiritual guidance.

Celebrations

Guru Gobind Singh's birthday is marked with a *gurpurb* very similar to that held on Guru Nanak's birthday. In India, the festival takes place on the day itself. In other countries, such as Britain, it is usually celebrated on the nearest Sunday. In Britain, the roads are sealed off so that a procession of the *Panj Piare* and the Guru Granth Sahib can take place. The procession passes by the local *Gurdwaras*, which are decorated with banners and flowers.

Celebrations for Guru Gobind Singh's birthday in London.

Karah parshad

Karah parshad is a sweet pudding shared at the end of Sikh services. To make *karah parshad*, you will need:

1 cup (250 ml) of sugar
1 cup (250 ml) of unsalted butter
1 cup (250 ml) of wheat flour
1/2 cup (125 ml) of water

1. Melt the butter in a saucepan over low heat.

2. Add the flour and cook for a few minutes until it is golden brown.

3. Mix in the sugar and water and stir until thick.

4. Allow to cool, then share with your friends.

Hola Mohalla

The festival of *Hola Mohalla*, which means "the place to attack," is celebrated in February or March at about the same time as the great Hindu spring festival of *Holi*. *Hola Mohalla* is a *jore mela*, a colorful, lively time in the Sikh calendar.

A Sikh dressed as a **Nihang**, *or Sikh warrior.* *Groups of* **Nihangs** *travel through the Punjab, taking part in festivals such as* **Hola Mohalla**.

How *Hola Mohalla* began

Hola Mohalla was begun in 1680 in the town of Anandapur, in northern India, by Guru Gobind Singh, the 10th Sikh Guru. He felt that the Hindu festival of *Holi* had become too frivolous and decided that the Sikhs should have their own festival on the day after *Holi*. He summoned the Sikhs together to practice the military skills they needed to defend their faith against the Mughal rulers. They brought their weapons, fought mock battles, and took part in military drills and parades as if they were on a real battlefield. At the end, Guru Gobind Singh led an attack on a model castle.

Celebrating *Hola Mohalla*

Today, *Hola Mohalla* is mainly celebrated in Anandapur, where it began. Thousands of Sikhs gather there to take part in the festival. After a morning service in the *Gurdwara*, there are displays of martial arts and sporting contests, such as swordsmanship, archery, wrestling matches, and horse riding. These are followed by music and poetry competitions. Hymn singing and religious talks take place in the presence of the Guru Granth Sahib. There is also a great parade, led by Sikhs dressed as the *Panj Piare* carrying the flags of the local *Gurdwaras*. *Hola Mohalla* is also celebrated by some Sikhs in Britain, the United States, and Canada.

A demonstration of martial arts at Hola Mohalla.

Kabaddi

Local sports competitions often take place around the time of *Hola Mohalla*. *Kabaddi* is an Indian game that is also played by many Sikhs. The word *Kabaddi* literally means "dividing an area into two halves."

There are two teams of players. The goal of the game is for one player to break through a row of members of the other team as they try to touch him or wrestle him to the ground. At the same time, he has to take a deep breath and repeat "*Kabaddi*" for as long as he can before taking another breath. As soon as he runs out of breath and takes another, he has to stop.

Baisakhi

On April 13th or 14th, Sikhs celebrate the festival of *Baisakhi*. At this time, they remember a very important event in Sikh history—the founding of the *Khalsa*, or Sikh community, by Guru Gobind Singh, the 10th Sikh Guru. The word *Baisakhi* comes from the name of the month in which the festival falls (see page 28). In India, *Baisakhi* also marks the start of the New Year for Sikhs, when the winter wheat crop was harvested.

Happy Baisakhi!

The story of *Baisakhi*

On *Baisakhi* in 1699, Guru Gobind Singh called the Sikhs together. About 20,000 Sikhs came to Anandapur, where the Guru lived. With his sword in his hand, Guru Gobind Singh asked if any of them were willing to die for their faith. Nobody replied. The Guru asked a second time. Still nobody replied. When he asked a third time, a man named Darya Ram stepped forward. The Guru took him to his tent and returned minutes later, his sword dripping with blood. The crowd was horrified. The Guru asked for another Sikh and led him into his tent. He repeated his question three more times, and three more brave men came forward.

The *Panj Piare*

Then, an amazing thing happened. Guru Gobind Singh led the five men out of his tent, alive and unharmed. Like the Guru, they were dressed in bright yellow robes, blue sashes, and yellow turbans. The Guru explained to the crowd that these five men had proved their courage by being ready to die for their faith. From now on, they would be called the *Panj Piare*—the five beloved ones. They were the first members of the *Khalsa*, the new community of Sikhs.

The Guru prepared **amrit**, a special mixture of sugar and water, for the *Panj Piare* to drink. Then the Guru drank *amrit* from the same bowl. This showed that everyone was equal in God's eyes. Afterwards, many other Sikhs came forward to join the *Khalsa*.

A painting of Guru Gobind Singh and the Panj Piare *at the founding of the* Khalsa.

Five Ks

At *Baisakhi*, Guru Gobind Singh asked all Sikhs who joined the *Khalsa* to wear five items. These are known as the Five Ks because they all begin with the letter "K" in the Punjabi language:

1. *Kesh*—uncut hair. This shows obedience and devotion to God. Men keep their hair wrapped in a turban.

2. *Kangha*—a small wooden comb. This keeps long hair tidy. It reminds Sikhs of the importance of order and honesty.

3. *Kara*—a steel bracelet worn on the right wrist. Its circular shape shows unity with God and the *Khalsa*.

4. *Kirpan*—a small ceremonial sword. This symbolizes courage and willingness to fight for justice.

5. *Kachera*—a special pair of shorts worn as underwear. They were originally worn in battle.

Celebrating Baisakhi

Baisakhi is celebrated by Sikhs all over the world. It is a *jore mela*, a time for Sikhs to come together and show their commitment to their faith. There are services in the *Gurdwara* with prayers, hymns, and talks, and an *Akhand Path* is held. Some places have street processions led by the *Panj Piare*.

A street procession at Baisakhi.

Joining the *Khalsa*

Baisakhi is a time when many young Sikhs join the *Khalsa* at a special *amrit* ceremony held in the Gurdwara. It is led by five people representing the *Panj Piare*. The people who are to enter the *Khalsa* bathe and put on the Five Ks. During the ceremony, they kneel and receive *amrit* in their cupped hands. They drink it five times. It is also sprinkled on their eyes and hair. They are then members of the *Khalsa* and promise to follow the teachings of the Gurus.

Stirring the amrit *mixture for the amrit ceremony.*

The *Nishan Sahib* flag

The Sikh flag flies outside every *Gurdwara*. At *Baisakhi*, the flagpole is taken down and cleaned, and the flag and flagpole coverings are replaced. The flag is called the **Nishan Sahib**, which means "respected flag." It is triangular and made from yellow cloth, with a black *khanda* symbol in the center. The *khanda* is made up of a double-edged sword that stands for God's power. Around it is a circle to show that God has no beginning or end. The two crossed swords on the outside symbolize earthly and spiritual power. The *Nishan Sahib* was given to the Sikhs by the sixth Guru, Hargobind, to lead them in battle.

Changing the Nishan Sahib *at* Baisakhi.

New names

When Sikhs join the *Khalsa*, they are given new names as instructed by Guru Gobind Singh. He wanted Sikhs to share a name to show that they belonged to the same family. Men take the name *Singh,* which means "lion" and represents courage. Women take the name *Kaur,* which means "princess" to show their important status.

A *Nishan Sahib*

You can make this flag any size you like.

1. Cut out a triangle of yellow cloth.

2. Cut out a *khanda* symbol from black cloth and pin or sew it on the triangle. It may be easier to make the symbol in pieces — the double-edged sword, the circle, and the two swords — then put it all together.

3. Fold the side of the triangle around a piece of dowel and glue it in place.

4. Make another *khanda* symbol from cardboard covered in aluminum foil. Glue this to the top of the flagpole.

A small khanda *symbol made from cardboard and foil.*

Guru Arjan Dev

In June, a *gurpurb* is held that marks the death of Guru Arjan Dev, the fifth Sikh Guru, in 1606. On this day, Sikhs remember how Guru Arjan Dev was put to death by the Mughal emperor Jahangir because he refused to give up his beliefs. Sikhs say that Guru Arjan Dev was the first Sikh martyr.

A painting of Guru Arjan Dev, who was put to death for holding to his religious beliefs.

Story of Guru Arjan Dev

Guru Arjan Dev became Guru in 1581 when he was 18 years old. At that time, India was ruled by Emperor Akbar, who was friendly toward the Sikhs. But when Akbar died, his son, Jahangir, a devout Muslim, became emperor instead. Jahangir did not like the Sikh religion because he thought that it was becoming too popular. When Jahangir found out that his rebellious son, Prince Khusro, had visited the Guru, he was furious. He believed that the Guru was plotting against him and ordered him to pay a huge fine. He also told him to change the words of the Guru Granth Sahib. Guru Arjan Dev refused to alter the holy book and said that he had money for only the poor and needy.

A terrible fate

Hearing this, Jahangir had the Guru arrested and locked up in prison in Lahore. Then he had the Guru tortured. For three days, the Guru was locked in a cell without food or water, even though it was summer and blazing hot. Over the next few days, he was put in a barrel of boiling water, had burning sand poured over him, and was made to sit on a red-hot iron plate. Even then, the Guru would not give in or complain. Finally, he was pushed into the river Ravi, where he drowned.

The river Ravi, where Guru Arjan Dev drowned.

Sikhs serving water to passers-by to mark Guru Arjan Dev's death.

Cool drinks

Sikhs mark Guru Arjan Dev's death by listening to stories about his life and death. It is also customary to set up roadside stations serving free, cold drinks to passers-by. This reminds Sikhs of the terrible thirst Guru Arjan Dev suffered as he was being tortured. The drinks also show that Sikhs have no hard feelings toward anyone and that no one should suffer as the Guru did. Looking out for others is very important to Sikhs. Handing out drinks is a way of serving people and God.

Divali

The third *jore mela* in the Sikh calendar is *Divali*, the festival of lights. It is celebrated in October or November by Sikhs all around the world. At *Divali*, Sikhs remember how the sixth Guru, Guru Hargobind, returned home to Amritsar after his release from prison.

Sikhs in London lighting candles for Divali.

The story of *Divali*

After Guru Arjan Dev's death, the Sikhs realized that they would have to fight to defend their faith. Guru Arjan Dev's son and successor, Guru Hargobind, began to train an army. This worried Emperor Jahangir. To find out more about it, he invited the Guru on a hunting trip. On this trip, Guru Hargobind saved the emperor's life when a tiger leaped out and attacked him. After this, the two men became friends. Then the emperor fell ill. He was told that he would recover only if a holy man prayed for him. So he asked the Guru to go to Gwalior Fort to pray for him. In the fort, Guru Hargobind was treated very well. But the fort was also a prison, and the 52 Hindu princes kept captive there were not so lucky. They had only rags to wear and very little to eat. The Guru tried to help them in any way he could.

Hindu *Divali*

Divali is one of the most important festivals of the year for Hindus. But it is celebrated by Hindus for a different reason. There are many stories associated with the Hindu *Divali* festival. One story tells of how the god Rama and his wife, Sita, returned from exile to be crowned king and queen. At *Divali*, Hindus light *diva* lamps to guide Rama and Sita home.

The Guru's cloak

Jahangir recovered from his illness and told the Guru that he was free to go. But the Guru refused to leave the fort unless the Hindu princes were also freed. Jahangir was horrified. He told the Guru that he could take as many princes as could hold on to his cloak when he left the fort. The emperor knew that the gateway was very narrow. He thought that the Guru would be able to take only four or five princes with him, but no more. But the Guru was even more clever. He had a cloak made with 52 long silk tassels, one for each of the princes. Then he walked out of the fort, taking all of the princes with him.

A painting of Guru Hargobind leading the Hindu princes out of Gwalior Fort.

The Golden Temple in Amritsar at Divali.

Celebrating Divali

When Guru Hargobind returned home to Amritsar after his release, the Sikhs decorated the Harimandir (Golden Temple) with lights to welcome him. Every year at *Divali*, the whole Golden Temple is again illuminated to remember this happy event. There are also fireworks displays. Many Sikhs light their homes with candles or small clay lamps called *divas* to welcome Guru Hargobind home. They also go to services in the *Gurdwara*, which is specially decorated for the occasion.

Festival Calendar

Month	Festival
October/November	Guru Nanak's birthday
November/December	Guru Tegh Bahadur's martyrdom
December/January	Guru Gobind Singh's birthday
February/March	*Hola Mohalla*
April 13/14	*Baisakhi*
June	Guru Arjan Dev's martyrdom
October/November	*Divali*

Sikh months

In the Hindu lunar calendar, the months are:

Magha	(January/February)
Phalguna	(February/March)
Chaitra	(March/April)
Vaisakha	(April/May)
Jyeshtha	(May/June)
Ashadha	(June/July)
Shravana	(July/August)
Badra	(August/September)
Ashvina	(September/October)
Karttika	(October/November)
Margashirsha	(November/December)
Pausha	(December/January)

In the *Nanakshahi* calendar, the months are:

Katik	(October/November)
Maghar	(November/December)
Poh	(December/January)
Magh	(January/February)
Phagan	(February/March)
Chet	(March/April)
Vaisakh	(April/May)
Jeth	(May/June)
Harh	(June/July)
Sawan	(July/August)
Bhadon	(August/September)
Asu	(September/October)

In the *Nanakshahi* calendar, the year begins in *Katik* with the birthday of Guru Nanak.

Glossary

Akhand Path — A nonstop reading of the Guru Granth Sahib that takes place at festivals and other special occasions.

Amrit — A special mixture of sugar and water used in Sikh ceremonies.

Amritsar — A city in the Punjab, India; it is the Sikhs' holiest city.

Devout — Very holy or religious.

Gurdwara — A building in which Sikhs meet to worship.

Gurmukhi — The script used for writing the Punjabi language.

Gurpurbs — Festivals that remember key times in the lives of the Sikh Gurus.

Guru — One of 10 great Sikh teachers who lived between 1469 and 1708.

Guru Granth Sahib — The holy book of the Sikhs.

Hindu — A follower of (or something related to) the Indian religion of Hinduism.

Hinduism — An ancient religion that began in India at least 4,000 years ago. It is still followed by most Indians.

Islam — The religion of the Muslims. Muslims form the second biggest religious group in India. The Mughal rulers of India were Muslims.

Jore melas — Joyful festivals that celebrate important events from Sikh history.

Karah parshad — A sweet pudding that is shared at the end of Sikh services and ceremonies.

Khalsa — The Sikh community begun by Guru Gobind Singh in 1699. The word *Khalsa* means "pure."

Langar — A meal that everyone shares at the end of a Sikh service. It is also the name of the room in the *Gurdwara* where the meal is prepared and served.

Martyrdom — The death of someone who dies for his or her faith.

Muslim — A follower of (or something related to) the religion of Islam.

Nishan Sahib — The Sikh flag that flies above all *Gurdwaras*.

Panj Piare — The first five members of the *Khalsa*.

Punjab — The region of northwest India where Sikhism began.

Sewa — The Sikh belief in helping other people as a way of serving God.

Shabads — Hymns found in the Guru Granth Sahib.

Further Resources

Books

Dhanjal, Beryl.
Sikhism.
New York: Peter Bedrick Books, 2002.

Ganeri, Anita.
Storyteller: Sikh Stories.
London: Evans Brothers, 2001.

Panesar, Rajinder Singh.
Guru Nanak and Sikhism.
North Mankato, Minn.: Smart Apple Media, 2002.

Singh, Nikky-Guninder Kaur.
Sikhism.
New York: Facts on File, 1993.

Web Sites

http://www.festivals.com
Information about festivals, holy days, and holidays.

http://www.sikhs.org
Information about all aspects of Sikhism.

http://www.allaboutsikhs.com
More facts about Sikhs and their religion.

http://www.indiancultureonline.com
Details about how Sikh festivals are celebrated in India.

Index